FROM NORFOLK TO NORMANDY

Alan Marshall and Juliet Webster

Published in Great Britain in 2016 by Mascot Media, Norfolk.
Email: mascot_media@btinternet.com   Web: www.mascotmedia.co.uk

© Mascot Media Ltd.

Illustrations: © Julian Cory-Wright Collection.

A CIP catalogue record for this book is available from the British Library.

ISBN: 978-0-9954651-2-1

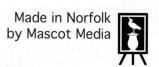

**Made in Norfolk
by Mascot Media**

Scanning by Hussey Knights, Norwich (www.husseyknights.co.uk). Image processing by Alan Marshall for Mascot Media.

Photographs by Sir Geoffrey Cory-Wright, unless indicated otherwise.

Research and writing by Juliet Webster and Alan Marshall.

Designed by Alan Marshall. Edited by Marion Scott Marshall.

Printed by Swallowtail Print, Drayton Industrial Park, Taverham Road, Drayton, Norwich, Norfolk NR8 6RL.
Email: contact@swallowtailprint.co.uk   Web: www.swallowtailprint.co.uk

All images by Julian Cory-Wright, unless indicated otherwise. Front cover: (top) Brancaster Harbour and Marshes; (bottom) Normandy convoy, June 1944.
Back cover: (background) 18th Green from the 19th, Royal West Norfolk Golf Club; (left) Julian with his dog Emma at Brancaster; (top right) Brancaster Dial House and Barn;
(bottom right) 60-pounder field gun emplacement, RA training.

Title page: Brancaster from Scolt Head Island, oil, February 1944. Page 2 (background): The Ship Cottage, Brancaster. Facing page: Julian sketching at Solva, South Wales.

Dedication

For Julian's five grandchildren, and his four and future great-grandchildren.

Julian Cory-Wright 1916-1944

This story begins with an ending, and tells the tale of a short life bookended by war. Like so many of his generation, Anthony John Julian Cory-Wright (known to his family and friends as Julian) was born midway through the first truly global conflict, and was to lose his life less than three decades later as the Second World War entered its final stage.

Having attained the rank of Captain, 181 Field Regiment, Royal Artillery, Julian died in Normandy two months short of his 28th birthday. His two daughters were aged three and not yet two years of age when he was killed in action, while his son was just five months old.

His was an unlucky and lonely death on the Regiment's first day in battle. B-Troop Commander Cory-Wright with 177 Battery was killed on the morning of 26 June 1944. His small party was moving forward on foot to reconnoitre his forward observation position when a mortar bomb landed nearby. He is buried in the British Military Cemetery at Tilly-sur-Seulles.

The life cut short during the invasion of occupied France had been rich and varied, not least because the young officer was an excellent mathematician, as well as being remarkably skilled with pencil, paint brush and even linocutting tools.

While few artistic opportunities presented themselves during the landing in Normandy and its immediate aftermath, he had been able to record people and places encountered from his schooldays through office life and military training to his ill-fated departure from Tilbury Docks.

Loved greatly by his family and friends, the young artillery officer left not only a legacy of fond memories and the respect of colleagues, but the more tangible sketchbooks and paintings that helped chart his journey from the unspoilt coast of north-west Norfolk to the more hostile shoreline of northern France.

From Norfolk to Normandy not only provides a long-awaited showcase for a talent lost to war, but shares for the first time this personal testimony with a wider audience.

Alan Marshall, Sutton, Norfolk   *August 2016*

Gun-towing artillery tractor ('Quad'), RA training

Carnival, Wells-next-the-Sea, 1930

Above: a pencil sketch of Felicity Cory-Wright at her desk.
Right: Geoffrey Cory-Wright

From Norfolk to Normandy

Born in London and raised in the capital during the final two years of the First World War, Julian Cory-Wright would soon lose his heart to Norfolk's unspoilt north-west coast. As a child, he came to call several places 'home'. Term-times were spent boarding at his Surrey preparatory school and, later, Eton College, while holidays were taken at The Manor House in Knebworth or at the family retreat in Brancaster. It was the latter that he missed most when he was away at school and while studying accountancy in London and training to be an artillery officer in the war years.

Julian's birthplace was in London's All Souls Place, the home of his maternal grandmother. This was an attractive Regency building that was later demolished during the construction of the BBC's Broadcasting House. He arrived in August 1916 as the Battle of the Somme raged. His father Geoffrey, having fought in France as a Captain in the 3rd Battalion East Kent Regiment ('The Buffs'), was by then a Flight Commander in the Royal Flying Corps (RFC) in Mesopotamia.

Geoffrey Cory-Wright was from a family of industrialists. His father, Sir Arthur Cory-Wright, was Chairman of William Cory & Son, a large and successful coal factor with fleets of lighters on the Thames, as well as its own colliers and tugs. At the start of the Great War, the firm encouraged its workers to enlist, and they formed an entire company of the East Kent Regiment as a so-called pals' unit. Despite the priority of warship-building, Cory's managed to commission new tonnage in the war years, and a new ship was named 'The Buffs' in honour of the East Kent Regiment.

Following the 1914-1918 war, in which Geoffrey and his three brothers all saw active service, Geoffrey returned to the family business and divided his time between Powell Duffryn House in Cardiff and the London offices, Cory Buildings, in Fenchurch Street. The company continued to build and operate colliers between the wars. Geoffrey was therefore well versed in the management of coal transportation – expertise that would see him

employed during the Second World War by the Ministry of Fuel and Power in Nottingham and the Ministry of Mines in Northampton.

Geoffrey's wife, and Julian's mother, was Felicity Tree, daughter of the distinguished actor-manager Sir Herbert Beerbohm Tree and his wife Maud. Felicity was born at 77 Sloane Street, Chelsea, and was brought up in a mix of society and theatrical London life. She was educated at Queens College, Harley Street, where her mother had taught Classics and Greek. Felicity was well read, highly intelligent and appeared occasionally in charitable performances on her father's stage at His Majesty's Theatre.

As a young girl she preferred rushing around the theatre from pit to gallery with her childhood friend Diana Manners (later Lady Diana Cooper). Full of drive and energy, Felicity, who sometimes wished she had been born a boy, had inherited both her father's wit and his flaming auburn hair. Her love of sport, particularly watersports, enabled her to win medals for swimming, diving and life-saving.

The Tree family was friendly with Raymond and Margot Asquith, and Felicity on one occasion, when dining at 10 Downing Street, was seated next to Rupert Brooke. He recalled the occasion in one of his poems, "Would God were eating plover's eggs and drinking dry champagne with... six or seven Asquiths and Felicity Tree in Downing Street again".

At the start of the First World War, after a brief spell training at Barts Hospital, alongside Diana Manners, Felicity took a nursing post at the Hotel Majestic Military Hospital in Paris under Dr. Cecil Joll FRCS. On her return to London she continued with her nursing at the Princess Club Hospital, Jamaica Road, Bermondsey. Felicity wrote: "If my friends knew I was nursing where there was typhoid they would treat me like a leper. The patients are nearly all Australians and such darlings. They were bundled to England straight from Gallipoli on an old tramp ship with very few nurses on board. No wonder disease of every sort broke out among them."

When Geoffrey joined the newly formed RFC, Felicity, in order to

keep abreast of events, especially news of Geoffrey and his squadron, obtained a clerical position at the Air Ministry, housed in the Hotel Cecil in the Strand. She held this post until the end of the War, and for her work in that connection she was Mentioned for Valuable Services.

Geoffrey and Felicity had married in November 1915, with Julian arriving in August the following year. He was soon accompanying his parents on holidays to the coastal village of Brancaster, with the enchanting Scolt Head Island nature reserve nestling close to the shore and its sandy beaches stretching four miles between the harbours of Brancaster Staithe and Burnham Overy Staithe.

He was the eldest of five boys, with the youngest, Mark, born in 1930 and thus 14 years Julian's junior. Michael was born in 1920; and the twins, David and Jonathan, joined the family in 1925. They had an idyllic childhood in and around Brancaster, Burnham Overy Staithe and Scolt Head Island, adding sailing and golf to swimming and beach games as they grew older.

Even as a child, Julian's artistic intent and prowess was evident. An early influence was Beerbohm Tree's half-brother, Max (later Sir Max) Beerbohm, the celebrated English essayist, parodist and caricaturist. He first became known in the 1890s as a dandy and a humourist, and was drama critic for *The Saturday Review* from 1898 until 1910. His caricatures, drawn usually in pen or pencil with muted watercolour tinting, can be found in many public collections.

Young Julian complained that he got to see his Uncle Max "far too infrequently" (not helped by Beerbohm's temporary relocation to Italy), but the cartoons and caricatures he produced from an early age suggest an appreciation and understanding of his uncle's work.

Geoffrey was a talented draughtsman himself, but his work meant he had limited involvement in his eldest son's enthusiasm for the visual arts. However, he enjoyed greatly

The Ship Cottage, London Street, Brancaster. Opposite: linocut book plate

Window, The Manor House, Knebworth

his own visits to Brancaster, being very knowledgeable about the wildlife and spending time watching birds on the marshes and on Scolt Head Island. A gifted amateur photographer, he turned professional following the Second World War, doing commercial work for the advertising agency J. Walter Thompson and contributing a sequence of 11 outstanding photographs to James Laver's 1951 book on Norfolk's Holkham Hall.

Felicity, as a young girl, had been sent from London to Brancaster for holidays, accompanied by her younger sister Iris and a succession of governesses. She had therefore developed strong links with the area before the war, and it was no surprise that the village was chosen as a home for her own family.

With the birth of their sons, Felicity persuaded Geoffrey to settle by the sea, at The Ship Cottage (see page 9) in Brancaster's London Street. The property, rented from the local Wordingham family, landlords of 'The Ship', was created from four adjoining premises (one a former grocery shop) and was surprisingly substantial – accommodating the five boys, their parents, nanny and a governess. In a tribute to the house's partly commercial origins, the Cory-Wrights referred to their long, refectory-style dining room that looked out on London Street as "the shop".

Helping raise and entertain the boys during their time at Brancaster was Nanny Annie Rees from the Mumbles area of South Wales – she remained with the family until her death in 1948. Miss Olive Scrivener (Scrivvy) was the family governess, who had also formed a deep affection for the boys. Her role was vital to the Cory-Wright household, involving driving the car, running numerous errands, and organising and joining in the various entertainments for the children.

With other London families descending upon Brancaster during the summer, complete with nannies and governesses, there was a large seasonal community that congregated on the beaches for picnics, games and swimming. Many of these friendships were to last a lifetime.

For Julian, life away from Brancaster was taken up by education, and he boarded initially at Sandroyd preparatory school, established in Cobham, Surrey, as a 'feeder' school for pupils destined for Eton. By the time Julian was at Sandroyd, it was being run by Messrs Wilson and

Hornby in purpose-built premises with good sports facilities. With the threat of war in 1939, the school relocated to the Wiltshire/Dorset borders and was attended there by the youngest of the Cory-Wright brothers, Mark. Enrolled as a 13-year-old boarder at Eton in September 1929, Julian went on to excel in mathematics, proved handy on the cricket pitch and showed early signs of promise as an artist.

At Eton, Julian is believed to have attended the drawing classes run by Wilfrid Jasper Walter Blunt (1901-1987), art teacher, author, artist and later curator of the Watts Gallery in Compton, Surrey. Present at Eton between the mid-1930s and 1959, he is famed for starting a revolution in the handwriting of British school children, using the 15th-century Italian Cancellaresca (Chancery) script as a basis.

Sharing Julian's passion for art at Eton was Toby Wake (Sir Hereward Wake), born in the same year and a rival for the Harmsworth Memorial Drawing Prize (which he won, while admitting that Julian was the better draughtsman). Wake left Eton to attend Sandhurst Military College, joining the King's Royal Rifles and receiving the Military Cross in 1942. Wounded in North Africa, he was invalided out of the Regiment in 1947 as a Major.

While Toby Wake was set for a military career, he described Julian as one of the most "unwarlike" of people, with his "delightfully" untidy appearance "not unusual" for someone so artistic.

Julian's Eton years saw him develop an interest in the relatively new art form of linocutting. This method of relief printmaking allowed for inexpensive production of designs using the common household flooring material, some cutting tools and ink for creating a reverse impression of the image gouged out of the lino block. Julian took the time in 1934 to produce his own hand-made guide to the linocutting process (see page 157).

Sharing some characteristics of woodcuts, a long-established form of printmaking, linocuts had been made fashionable by Picasso and Matisse in the early 1900s. Linoleum was cheaper to make, and offered an easier surface to carve than wood and metal, especially when heated. Julian was to produce a series of prints of Norfolk and other favourite locations that could be used as greetings cards, as well as more abstract designs based on repeated use of linocut motifs.

Away from school and back in Brancaster, Julian displayed a fascination

The Colonnades, Eton College

Sailing boat at anchor, 1932. Inset, engraving from cigarette case presented by Felicity in 1925 to Brancaster fisherman Richard Everitt

for boats and sailing that became a time-consuming pastime as well as providing the subject matter for a great number of sketches and paintings. To the end of his life, he couldn't resist vessels of all shapes and sizes, as long as there was some water beneath them.

Felicity had taught her eldest son to sail, but in 1925 almost lost the nine-year-old and a friend Evie Martelli to the sea when their boat capsized. Scared of frightening the boy, Felicity chose not to cry for help. Fortunately, local fishermen including Richard Everitt and Willy Loose rowed out from Brancaster Staithe to rescue them. The Everitt family, who still live locally, have kept the prized engraved silver cigarette case (see inset left) given in appreciation by Felicity.

When not messing about on boats, Julian would be capturing them in watercolour or pencil in the sketchbook kept with his paints in a canvas bag attached permanently to his shoulder. He worked quickly in the field, using one book for drawings and another for paintings, with most of his pieces completed in just a few minutes. His speed and deft brushwork impressed his contemporaries, perhaps more used to artists finishing their work in a studio environment. Friends became accustomed to him producing his 'dirty little paint box' at the drop of a hat; Julian hated to waste any paint – often using a mussel shell as a palette.

His first job, however, had nothing to do with art. Having left Eton as a student in 1935, he returned briefly to teach mathematics. This led him to enrol as an articled clerk with auditors Deloitte, Plender, Griffiths & Co and to work in London. The firm handled the audit for three public schools, including Eton, so often recruited from their clients.

Geoffrey and Felicity in the early 1930s decided to move out of London to the country. They responded to a notice from the Knebworth Estate Office in Hertfordshire that described The Manor House, in the confines of Knebworth Deer Park: "This fine old house, a Dower House on the Estate, is to be let. It is surrounded by lovely old grounds including tennis and croquet lawns, rose gardens, etc, and comprises hall, dining and drawing rooms, ten bedrooms, two bathrooms, kitchen, servants' hall, butler's pantry and other conveniences. Stabling and double garage. Rent £220 a year."

Knebworth is within easy reach of London and not too arduous a journey to Brancaster, so The Manor House became the hub of family life away

from the Norfolk coast. Knebworth Park, with its wide open spaces, lake and its 'wilderness', were painted regularly by Julian. On joining Deloitte's, he was able to commute daily from Hertfordshire into the City.

The accountancy firm had a policy of encouraging members of staff to join the Territorial Army (TA). Julian enlisted into the Hertfordshire Yeomanry, a reserve artillery unit, in a move that would have significant ramifications.

This particular regiment, with roots extending back to the late 18th century, specialised in artillery and first served during the Boer War. Julian was clearly destined to become a gunner from that point, with the Hertfordshire Yeomanry later redesignated and incorporated into the Royal Artillery. TA artillery regiments had a regular army adjutant, regimental sergeant major and a small number of senior non-commissioned officers (NCOs) as 'permanent staff'.

As Julian acquired the skills and experience for a career in accounting, he still found time to sketch and paint the architecture around him, The Thames and its shipping, and locations visited when on audit duties. He would use the vantage point of client buildings to get a good view of the surrounding area, resulting in a series of accomplished drawings.

The transformation of sailor and budding artist to accountancy professional continued as he passed his Preliminary Chartered Accountancy exams in July 1935, followed by the Intermediate exams three years later. His life in London meant more paintings and drawings of the capital, with Julian applying for permission from the Port of London Authority to paint in the London docks. The condition attached was that he should show them his work before exhibiting or publishing it.

Julian's birthdays were celebrated in Brancaster during the summer holidays, where he indulged his passions for walking (usually with his poodle Emma), sailing, playing golf at the Royal West Norfolk Golf Club and, of course, painting.

By then, he had his own sloop-rigged dinghy named 'Tam O'Shanter'

that he had bought from Burnham Overy Staithe resident Captain Woodgett – the last skipper of the famed tea clipper 'Cutty Sark' that nowadays resides on the Thames riverside at Greenwich. The boat's name resonates all the more because Julian's eventual posting to 181 Field Regiment and 15th Scottish Division meant he would wear that particular form of headgear.

In 1936, Julian acquired the 12-foot 'Sanderling', a National-class sailing boat built in Cambridge by H.C. Banham. The 'Sanderling' and her skipper entered regattas and open meetings throughout North Norfolk, while Julian produced a thesis on single-handed small boat sailing. He also blended his sailing and accountancy skills to become Hon. Auditor of the newly formed Brancaster Staithe Sailing Club, which in 1937 was given the Cory-Wright Cup.

Above: low tide at Brancaster. Facing page: watercolour sketch for possible linocut

Windsor Castle, 1936. Painted while back at Eton helping carry out an audit for Deloitte, Plender, Griffiths & Co

Newhaven Harbour, 1937

"The practice of sailing boats single-handed is an education in itself," Julian wrote in his thesis. *"The sailor learns to trust in himself and in the gear of his one-man craft. In order to be quite sure that his gear is worthy of his trust, he must see to it that this management of his boat is not merely limited to steering and handling the sheets. Only in this manner does a boat become a thing of great affection and, no matter what sort of craft they may be, the proud owners will boast about their capabilities, and their beauty and lines.*

"Caution and careful judgement comes but slowly to the would-be mariner, and only practise and experience will give him confidence, and greater ability. In sailing a boat single handed whether on the sea, in an estuary, or up a large river, local knowledge results, and conditions of wind and tide are learnt. In this way the sailor masters his art and from thence he attends less to his sheets and trim of his sails. For sheets and sails arrange themselves under the master's eye.

"Then, you may say, after that where lies the fascination of sailing, particularly by oneself? But this is only the beginning of the true game; less to attend to in the boat means that the senses can be directed to watching the sea and its moods, smelling the salt air, feeling wind on the cheeks, and hearing the roar of the waves which always roll along the coast or listening to the wild cry of gulls or wildfowl returning at sunrise or sunset from their feeding grounds. The signs are never the same and the more days spent in this pleasant contemplation of the sea, the greater is the wish for a longer life and more the wonder at nature."

Julian was as bewitched by art as by sailing, and in July 1937 he and a similarly culturally minded friend Martin Russell (also an Eton boy, who went on to become a successful investment banker and a champion for Sri Lankan art) travelled by train to Bavaria and Austria. Unable to get a sleeper compartment, they spent a night in Cologne, then travelled on to Munich.

Here they viewed many Old Masters at the Alte Pinakothek, one of the oldest art galleries in the world and housing a vast collection of works from the 14th to 18th centuries. They also tried to see the Neue Pinakothek with its collection of 19th-century art, but it was closed for cleaning. Julian noted that they did see some lovely woodcuts while in Munich.

They then moved south to Berchtesgaden, the beautiful Bavarian

Solva, South Wales. With Geoffrey working largely in Cardiff, family holidays were sometimes spent in Wales. The photograph on page 3, of Julian painting, was taken by his father at Solva while working on this picture. Facing page: King's Lynn, September 1936

Wolfgangsee, Austria, 1937. Facing page: Rex Whistler's poster design for Felicity's 'Fresh Flowers' shop

Alpine valley near the Austrian border (and nowadays a national park). Ironically, given Julian's eventual fate, this was a popular holiday destination for German Chancellor Adolf Hitler during the 1920s. He had bought a house in the Obersalzberg above the town, and other Nazi Party leaders were soon to frequent the region. The Kehlsteinhaus (also known to Allied troops as the Eagle's Nest) was built in the area for Hitler's 50th birthday in 1939.

Julian and Martin visited the picture-perfect Maria Gern pilgrimage church, which stands against the magnificent backdrop of the Watzmann mountain – the third highest in Germany and renowned for the rock-climbing challenges of its east face. Julian painted the interior of the church and its 18th-century altar on grey sugar paper (used often as a cheap and convenient medium by artists).

The young men's rail journey then took them over the border and into Austria at Salzkammergut, the equivalent of Britain's Lake District. Here Julian painted the landscape at Strobl and the Wolfgangsee – one of the country's 76 stunning lakes.

It was not only foreign landscapes that inspired Julian's art. Commissioned as a Second Lieutenant, 343 Battery, 86th Field Brigade in the Royal Regiment of Artillery – Territorial Army on 18 August 1937, he continued to join his TA unit at regular intervals and to visit different parts of the British Isles while training. One TA summer camp took him to Newhaven Harbour, where he painted his favourite subject, fishing boats. Other painting excursions prior to the outbreak of war saw Julian visit Pembrokeshire in Wales and Clovelly in Devon, where he continued to develop a large portfolio of watercolour landscapes.

It is difficult to know where the combination of professional accounting, accomplished sailing and artistic ability would have led Julian had not the shadow of war spread over Europe and enveloped Britain. Not at all warlike in temperament, he had however served effectively with the TA, and in September 1939 was mobilised with his younger brother Michael as part of the 86th (East Anglian) Field Regiment, Royal Artillery. Julian was among 66 men called up from Deloitte, Plender, Griffiths.

The outbreak of war meant the TA was 'embodied'. Both regular and TA units were mobilised and brought to their War Establishment strength including regular reservists being posted to TA units, which also absorbed their regular army permanent staff. The new National Service Act merged the regular army, TA, reserves and militia. It also made all men between 18 and 41 liable for conscription.

Julian was ranked Second Lieutenant in 341 (St Albans) Battery, stationed initially at Westleton in Suffolk. Close to the resort towns of

Southwold and Walberswick, he was able to take 'Sanderling' with him and continue to sail while helping defend the East Coast from the very real threat of German invasion.

Towards the end of the year, as winter descended, he wrote that he had sailed 'Sanderling' out at Walberswick, braving submerged German mines. "Just a little wind to beat the ebb which sets up to the North and back again, and made an expert landing and trailed home in the dark and 'Sanderling' now lies in a warm dry garage."

To some extent, Julian was lucky as the Regiment was to remain in Britain until 1944, being attached to various divisions. It only became absorbed into the British Second Army in 1944, forming part of the renowned 50th Infantry Division that saw action in Normandy and all major European campaigns leading up to the German surrender in 1945.

At the outbreak of war Felicity wrote to Julian and Michael from Brancaster: "We are all working very hard here – except Mark and the twins, who seemed stunned, poor darlings, at the sudden cessation of golf competitions, sailing, Weatherby noises and all the usual Brancaster atmosphere. On Sunday we had a very short service so as to hear the Prime Minister at 11.15. I knew what must be coming but how wonderful he was and how wonderful the King has been and everyone that has spoken of England and why we are fighting and what we are fighting for. It seems as if we are really saving the things my friends died for, which we all know in our heart of hearts are the only things that matter but which most of the world had cast aside since those days."

Equally momentous for Julian in 1939 was the meeting with his future wife, Susan Elwes, who had connections to his family and her own strong links with Norfolk – her father Bob lived at Congham. Susan herself was working in London in the Mayfair flower shop 'Fresh Flowers' owned and run by Julian's mother Felicity, who had set it up in the 1920s with Lady Diana Cooper. The shop boasted a poster designed by Rex Whistler – who was also to die in Normandy following the Allied landings, coincidentally less than three miles from where Julian was killed.

A popular haunt for visiting and local celebrities, 'Fresh Flowers' was also visited frequently by Julian in pursuit of a buttonhole. Stock was grown largely by Felicity at the family home in Knebworth or on her Brancaster allotment. She was a familiar sight in Mayfair, driving a grey Ford van filled with fresh flowers on the way to her shop. It was on account of her market gardening enterprise that during the war years Felicity was able to obtain extra petrol coupons.

At the outbreak of war Susan left the flower shop and Felicity, and joined the Auxiliary Territorial Service (ATS) at Chelsea Barracks with her younger sister Nancy. Her relationship with Julian blossomed, and in January 1940 they were engaged. Marriage wasn't seen by either family as a sensible option, given the outbreak of war, Julian's military service and modest Army pay. They were warned that they wouldn't be able to set up a proper home, and both sets of parents advised them to wait. Julian, writing to his mother in April 1940, said:

"Do you really think that life would be any sweeter and easier after the war? Don't you think Susan and I are capable of making a romance in this war? How can one tell how long this should last? I sound impatient and headstrong and foolish, but we are young people who are marrying – not middle-aged such as govern the country today and with their lack of imagination and foresight, courage and strength have brought us to this sorry pass."

Choosing a date and even guaranteeing the groom's availability for the wedding became increasingly difficult as the political situation deteriorated and the fear of imminent invasion rose. In April 1940, by which time Julian's unit was stationed in Northumberland, he wrote home that: "We are all recalled from leave and no one is allowed off. We are even confined to barracks. I am standing by now to wait for parachutists – this sort of thing is very likely between dusk and dawn. It is now nearing 10 o'clock and it is not dusk yet. We are expecting anything and have to be prepared."

There were supporters of an early wedding, in spite of the challenges. Joan Evershed, a Brancaster neighbour, and wife of Sir Raymond Evershed, a prominent judge and later Master of the Rolls, wrote: "You seem a most perfectly matched pair, and I do hope you will find great happiness together. Brancaster was not itself at New Year without the Cory-Wright family in its entirety, but it did its best and it was heaven being there after months here in London. Clara and Maud made us so comfortable at The Ship and the marshes looked perfect in the frost and sunshine."

The Bishop of St. Albans, Michael Furse, was another staunch upholder of the planned marriage, and wrote: "I am very glad this

Dunstanburgh Castle, Northumberland, 1940. Facing page: Susan Cory-Wright as sketched by Julian

BELSAY GARDEN

happiness has come to you, especially in these dark and difficult days. For it will make I know all the difference to you both. It's a great adventure (so is the War and so is life itself) and one which makes the biggest demands upon all that we've got to give and that is why it is so well worth doing and doing well."

Uncle Max Beerbohm, writing to Felicity from his cottage near Dorking, wished he could come to Norfolk for the wedding. He wrote: "I'm quite well, nothing the matter with me physically: merely lacking in vitality, in going-power and staying power. But this defect, unimportant tho' it is, would make me an unsatisfactory wedding-guest, and I shall have to drink the health of the bride and bridegroom on these little premises. I do wish the world weren't in such an awfully tragic and threatening and threatened condition and that there were nothing to jar on marriage bells. But all the same I feel very glad the two young lovers are going to have their heart's desire. It's a bright patch to me in the midst of all the gloom."

Perhaps most poignantly, Max's sister, Dora Beerbohm, a nun in St. Saviour's Priory, sent a telegram to Felicity on 28 May: "I am dying. One sees then very clearly what is right. I feel that Julian and Susan should marry at once. Please let this be. Auntie Dora, London Hospital, Whitechapel." Dora died in August 1940, her wish having been granted.

On 25 May, Julian again wrote to his mother from Northumberland. "I saw the Colonel this morning. He said that there was no hope of getting leave while army leave was stopped as a whole and also while we were on six hours' notice to go and defend the post allotted to us." However, the commanding officer eventually gave permission, and a wedding date of 1 June 1940 was set.

Julian was given 48 hours' leave to be married quietly at Congham church in Susan's home village. The reception, however, was held at Castle Rising: Susan's father and his second wife were living at the Mill House there because their home – Congham House – had been burned to the ground on the night of 17 November 1939. Susan and her sister Nancy had lost everything they possessed except for a small suitcase of clothes they had with them in London, and their ATS uniforms.

Following the reception at the Mill House, the honeymoon of two nights was spent at Valley Farm, Brancaster Staithe, lent for the occasion by Bill Simms-Adams and his glamorous French wife Gaby, who added some 'chic' to Brancaster life.

Julian rejoined the regiment at Wildrington, near Morpeth, on the Northumberland coast, with Susan staying nearby at Belsay with friends the Pumphrey family. There was plenty to paint up in the wild north-east, with deserted beaches and the Holy Island of Lindisfarne. The artist

Four pictures painted in the late summer of 1940 when Susan was with Julian on a four-day trip to Ennerdale in the Lake District.
Facing page: a pencil drawing of Belsay Quarry Garden, Northumberland, completed during the same period

Holy Island (Lindisfarne)

also turned his hand to images of his unit and other military personnel.

One whole sketchbook is filled with pictures painted in the late summer of 1940 when Susan was with him on a four-day trip to Ennerdale, at the north-west corner of the Lake District.

"It is a wonderful part of the world. The peace of it is wonderful and not a sound," Julian wrote to his father. *"Here is a book of drawings, a book that I finished yesterday. It starts, if you begin the right end, with our trip to Cumberland, Ennerdale, the journey back, then a few sketches of local things and finally yesterday's visit to Dunstanburgh. It is wonderful country lying between Alnwick and the Farne Islands. Do come."*

At idle moments during exercises, he painted the military scene before him, with broken-down vehicles, map plotting, guns and towing quads, the firing ranges, troops on the road or at camp, fellow officers in the mess and soldiers operating wireless sets, command posts, soldiers leaning against trees or resting under haystacks.

In the late summer and autumn of 1940, the Northumberland coast was defended by 60-pounder field guns, relics with metal wheels from the 1914-1918 war. "We fired our guns today," Julian wrote, "very interesting. We were only firing into the sea." He painted one of these under camouflage surrounded by its sandbags. The guns, which had no towing vehicles and had to be loaded on to trains to be moved, stood pointing from the Northumberland coast in the direction from which the invasion was expected. Until the spring of 1941, the renamed 86th Field Regiment had to make do with a variety of the elderly 60-pounders before the arrival in the summer of modern 25-pounders that had wheels with rubber tires and could be towed to firing positions.

Writing to Felicity in September 1940, Julian explained that he was keeping up the sketching and painting:

"Susan and I had a glorious but windy day on Sunday looking at castles on the coast and at churches. We found the only nice church I have seen up here at Warkworth. Northumberland is full of castles but the churches less interesting.

"We think we go into winter quarters soon, but we are already in a nice farm house with H & C and all sorts of plumbing – but no electric light.

"It is wretched about leave being stopped. But better that than to be caught napping. There may be an attempt of some sort before the autumn gales. We have a good system here whereby one can take 24 hours off duty a fortnight, to get right away from York to Edinburgh.

"I hope you will let the twins go back. I feel the coast is no fit place for them for the next few weeks. After that we can all breathe easier, but not too easily. Egypt I feel is next – then what?

"All love to all at Brancaster from Julian."

As the immediate risk of German invasion faded following the Battle of Britain in 1940, Julian moved around the country as he continued his training and took part in many exercises. He was lucky enough to avoid overseas postings, which enabled him to see more of Susan and his family.

The School of Artillery had relocated to Larkhill on Salisbury Plain in 1919, and was expanded dramatically once war had been declared, with greatly increased responsibilities. While individual training was the main activity, the school also conducted short overnight test exercises for all regiments in the summer months. In addition, the school was responsible for supervising all practice camps in the UK as well as training staffs of higher artillery headquarters. It was also heavily involved in new equipment, both its design and trials.

In May 1941, Julian wrote from HQ Royal Artillery 54th Division Home Forces:

"I have just been down to Larkhill to watch John Tabor and the rest of them shooting their guns off. They all seemed in very good form. Wonderful days there now that summer has really started – we were on Salisbury Plain and very exposed. I got completely burnt with sun and wind.

"I went on a very long distance visit on Tuesday to a camouflage centre at Farnham where I found Fred Mayor [who owned an art gallery] as an instructor. We spent an interesting afternoon. The people of the centre who invent and develop camouflage are the only real enthusiasts I have come across for a long time. Mostly painters and artists turned soldiers – they live on the crest of the wave and are real people."

Welsh farmhouse on the Roman Road near the RA Sennybridge Training Camp (see facing page)

Between 8 and 22 June 1941, Julian's regiment was at the newly acquired RA Practice Camp, Sennybridge, near Brecon, using their 25-pounders. It was from here that Julian painted a series of Cilieni Valley watercolours when he took off on a motorcycle with his faithful dog Emma for a long day to paint the scenery of that beautiful Welsh valley.

The remote Cilieni River meanders southwards through the steep farmland of the Brecon Beacons and into the River Usk. Julian appears to have painted constantly, and his rapid 'en plein air' technique meant he could produce watercolor sketches at great speed. Some of these helped earn him supper, when some locals spotted him painting. He wrote to his father:

"I spent most of yesterday on a motor bike painting and exploring. Yesterday evening, having decided to forgo dinner and stay out late still painting, I was asked in by a kind farmer and wife returning from the village to have supper with them. Tiny dark little farmhouse, but very good cider, boiled bacon, bread and butter. They all gabbled away in Welsh, and then apologised for doing so. The farmer I could never understand anyhow whether he spoke Welsh or English, but his wife was alright. An enormous cheese press occupied one side of the room and the fireplace the other. They were sweet people and very thrilled that they had an officer to supper."

By then, Susan was back in Norfolk; their first child, Virginia, was born at Gaywood on the outskirts of King's Lynn in May 1941 and christened at Burnham Deepdale. Susan was hard at work on Viyella petticoats and a cot cover with a seaweed and shell pattern border designed by Julian.

In 1942, one of the most historic houses in Brancaster Staithe became home for them. The Hoe (like The Ship Cottage, rented from the Wordinghams) was a low, white house overlooking the marshes and the harbour, and had been a smugglers' ale-house in the 19th century. During the Second World War it was placed on a list of houses to be requisitioned as a look-out while there was fear of an invasion.

Big changes were afoot within the British Army and the Royal Artillery, in response to Field Marshal Bernard Montgomery's request for more guns and gunners. These were to have a direct bearing on Julian's career, training and active service. The first record of plans to create a new regiment appeared in January 1942, when it was disclosed that the 6th Battalion King's Shropshire Light Infantry (KSLI) was to be incorporated into 181 Field Regiment Royal Artillery. This was a disappointment for many in this proud infantry unit, but they were soon to become highly proficient with the 25-pounder field guns.

Royal Artillery Northern Commander Brigadier Wainwright visited KSLI on 14 February 1942 to begin the reshaping process – perhaps appropriately, using Valentine's Day to bring the two sides together.

Immediately they began looking for a suitable training ground, and swiftly chose Melton Mowbray in Leicestershire.

On 28 February 1942, 6th Battalion King's Shropshire Light Infantry ceased to exist. With immediate effect, 484 other ranks were reposted to 181 Field Regiment RA. KSLI officers were offered a choice of transferring, or reposting to other infantry units. Eighteen of them chose to stay with the new unit, of whom just nine were left when the Regiment sailed for France in June 1944.

The priority was now bringing the new Regiment up to strength, and this was achieved largely through the reposting of RA personnel. By 10 March 1942, more than 30 officers and NCOs had joined. The former KSLI officers were sent to artillery training school for a crash course, with the captains assigned to Larkhill, before rejoining the Regiment in August. The experienced artillery officers back at Melton Mowbray got on with retraining the other ranks and taking delivery of guns, vehicles and other equipment. Julian joined just five days after the conversion. He was Assistant Adjutant, then Adjutant, and later became a Troop Commander. Lieutenant Colonel E. O. Herbert was the first commander of 181 Field Regiment. Later, Lt. Col. Archie Devereux took over and led the Regiment, with Julian then Adjutant.

The Regiment was reorganised into three training batteries, each made up of three troops. After a couple of months, one troop from each training battery was reposted to form three permanent batteries. An artillery field regiment had 24 guns (25-pounders), vehicles, workshops and an establishment of 672 of all ranks. Three 8-gun batteries were divided into two 4-gun troops. There were 204 officers and men in these batteries, each commanded by a major. The troops were each

commanded by a captain – one of whom would shortly be Julian. Following the reorganisation, the new Regiment moved north to the moorlands of West Yorkshire to perfect its shooting skills.

In November 1942, it was agreed that 181 Field Regiment RA was to become the only English artillery regiment of the reformed 15th Scottish Division. It wasn't until July 1943 that 181 actually joined up with the enlarged Division.

Major Dudley Shaw, who joined 181 from the KSLI, described the new Regiment as "the oddest of gunners". They wore the distinctive green lanyards of a Light Infantry Regiment and Scottish bonnets with a gunner's badge (a bomb) and the emblem of the 15th Scottish Division. This was the Scottish Lion Rampant in a circle, representing an 'O' (the 15th letter of the alphabet). Added to that was the bugle of the KSLI, since most of 181 was made up of officers and men of that infantry regiment – although Julian had of course come originally from the Hertfordshire Yeomanry.

Below left: Brancaster with the sailing boat 'Amity', involved in the Dunkirk evacuation. Below right: Julian at Brancaster Staithe, summer 1943. He is standing beside the Southerland wash pit – each mussel fisherman had his own pit where the mussels were washed. Cyril Loose's 1937-built whelk boat, 'The Isabel', is in the background. Facing page: Royal Artillery ranges, Sennybridge RA Training Camp, June 1941

When Julian was back at the School of Artillery at Larkhill in May 1942, he took the opportunity to visit his youngest brother, Mark, then aged 12, at Sandroyd – now relocated to the Wiltshire/Dorset border. Julian wrote from Larkhill: "I have just got back here from seeing Mark. I fear it was rather dull for him. Apart from bringing him a few stamps that I had found for him in Salisbury, at which he seemed very pleased, I brought nothing. Mr. Ozanne [the school's owner and Headmaster] talked to me about Common Entrance. Mark's maths is good but not sufficiently brilliant at the moment to produce a scholarship. Mr. Ozanne very kindly took me back to the bus stop [saving Julian the return four-mile walk to Amesbury Bus Station]."

In August 1942, Julian was back in Northumberland at Redesdale, No 5 Practice Camp. "The summer here," he wrote, "is nearly gone and I never heard the Curlew which up till June is alive all over the moors. I am only just outside Newcastle, but the country is lovely all round. This week we are practising in the Cheviots, Redesdale range. It has poured with rain all day but I feel better for being out here compared with Gosforth."

The Cory-Wrights had been worrying about the fate of their second son, Michael, since the fall of Singapore. Julian, in a late 1942 letter, asked: "Did you know Michael was a Captain some time ago? His name has just appeared in War Office Orders as War Substantive Lieutenant to be temporary Captain with effect from July 1942. I have no idea what this implies regarding his posting as missing or not. What is the latest news that you heard?" More than a year passed before there was a message through The Vatican that Michael was 'safe' as a prisoner of the Japanese in Thailand.

October 1942 saw the birth of Julian and Susan's second daughter, Juliet, this time at The Hoe that had become their home at Brancaster Staithe. Visits home to Brancaster for Julian during this period were limited to a few days' leave from his intensive army life for occasions such as the children's christenings.

In January 1943, the three 181 batteries were given their final designations: 177 (Julian's unit), 178 and 179. At this point they were stationed at Longframlington and Ross Links in Northumberland. The batteries exercised all over the Yorkshire moors. Regimental HQ moved to Haydon Bridge, Northumberland, in April 1943. The 15th Scottish Division was told in September 1943 that it was to be a spearhead Division of VIII Corps of the British Second Army. It was the only mixed infantry division, with the

'My tank troubles'

Wearing the Tam O'Shanter

Jeep leading a convoy of Quads

Richard Hargreaves

other two being Armoured Divisions. Training therefore began with tanks. The Regiment moved to Ripon and Boroughbridge in Yorkshire, while Regimental HQ moved to the Hildebrand Barracks in Harrogate.

Exercises were tough, sometimes harsh and very hard going. On one competitive exercise officers each took a squad of men with rations for one day marching from one village in Northumberland to another, across mountains and moorland by the quickest possible route. Most of them tried to follow tracks or paths marked on the map. Julian, with his squad, won easily because he was bold enough to follow the contours on the map and so saved a lot of energy.

In December 1943, Julian was at Hildebrand Barracks and wrote from there to his mother:

"I feel sure this must be Bronte country as out to the west it is wild and bitterly cold at times. We have had two falls of snow on the links, not thick enough to ski but they stayed for several days. Harrogate is fairly high up too and we were exposed to the seven winds of Hell. I wear a fleece sheepskin waistcoat under my battle dress and a balaclava is ideal. Do you think you could find my old skiing mittens, leather ones, that keep out everything that comes their way?

"You will find my tank troubles in the midst of the Yorkshire moors on the other side of this [Julian had sketched the scene on the back of his letter – it is shown on page 32]. We got it going in the end."

To his brother Jonathan (who with his twin, David, had left school in July that year and were both immediately issued with call-up papers) Julian wrote:

"We have just got back from two days on the coast [likely to have been Speeton Gap near Filey] though I never saw the sea and did not hear it either — we arrived too late at night to see it. The following day we were due to shoot out to sea. We slept in a deserted coastguard cottage high up above the local village. A gale was blowing and it was pitch dark finding one's way up to bed. Even by night we could feel the sea was not very far away. But we were up before it was light enough to see how near the cliff edge really was.

"We stood all day in the same wind blowing from the south; all the targets were knocked down by the force of the gale and we got very little shooting done. Also, the fishing boats were sheltering under the cliff so we were stopped from firing for quite a long time. We gave it up about three o'clock and went back to get some dinner. The only good thing about our trip to the sea was a splendid fire in a farmhouse where we had supper the previous night.

"We rattled home in pitch dark all through York, with its very narrow and twisty streets, and got home about ten o'clock at night. We travelled very fast. I rode a motor bicycle most of the way. When I got in I might well have been sunbathing in the South of France for a week from the colour of my face I had had so much wind.

"Do let me know how you are getting on. How long do you spend at your OCTU before you get your commission? I know it varies so much with the branch of the Army."

Julian was still at Hildebrand Barracks on New Year's Eve 1943 and had spent Christmas there. He wrote to his father:

"Christmas was rather a flop here from my own point of view, though I tried some

Training — pulling vehicles out of a river in practice for the Normandy landings

gaiety but it wore thin rapidly. I did go to Ripon Cathedral on Sunday and was in the belfry to watch them peal the bells. I have an NCO who is very keen on this and he went over specially to peal the bells. The service was rather remote in that vast place and I was a long way back.

"The men's dinner was a terrific affair. Feeding the 600 and making them drink too. All the officers and sergeants helped as well — hindered chiefly. It was fun at the time. We ate our own Christmas dinner on Sunday night. This was quite a peacetime celebration and ended up at the sergeant's mess dance about half past one in the morning. Unfortunately every party leaves me more certain that I don't want another,

yet we all go to the next. I did have the most excellent meal (sorry to harp on the meals all the time, but such is Christmas fare) at a little pub way out towards the moors and right on top of the world. The dinner is always the same, yet nothing could be more exciting as it consists of huge thick slices of ham, fried, with eggs followed by real ice creams! The landlord makes a collection of all sorts of odd wines and spirits from local sales, and though he passes these fantastic prices on, it is one of the few places near here where you can name your drink and your liqueur and be certain of getting it.

"Golden plover abound in the field next door to the camp. Several were shot the other day by one or two of the officers – I was not in on the battle. They were cooked beautifully last night by a staff sergeant instructor who is here to teach the mess staff how to cook. He revels in the name of 'Joseph'. That's his surname – he came from the Ritz before the war: a superb man, very good disciplinarian and a wonderful cook.

"The war cannot be long now, but how I long to get on with myself. We are all feeling keyed up to do something, but it's dreadful sitting and waiting. We're busy, not as busy I think we ought to be. No drive, no push, yet everyone is keen. I cannot make it out. I have at last got two ideal subalterns, one a mountain of energy, five foot six tall; and one other very keen member, rather argumentative, but otherwise alright. All my love to you all at home, Julian."

The following day, New Year's Day 1944, Julian wrote to his mother:

"'Eheu Phugaces labuntur anni' – to quote from Horace, one of the few snippets of Latin that I managed to remember, despite oceans of authors that were thrust into my hands. Horace says, talking to Phugaces, a friend, 'Alas, Phugaces, the years slip by'. Just so, another year, but full of glory for so many. I feel I have missed this glory, nor does it feel right and proper to be thankful in the shadow of the glory of others. I think you are very right when you say that my four years of waiting have been hard. I must keep up to scratch though, at this time especially. To fall away now into the ruts that lie all around me would be to waste the whole of the last four years."

In January 1944, Julian's son Richard was born at The Hoe in Brancaster. Susan had visited her parents-in-law earlier that day, and owing to the petrol shortage walked back to Brancaster Staithe in the snow wearing an old pair of flying boots. It was hardly surprising that the baby arrived before Doctor Devlin had time to get there. Richard, christened in February 1944, was given the second name Michael after Julian's younger brother who was still interred in a Japanese POW camp.

In Britain, there were a number of courses officers had to attend in that lengthy

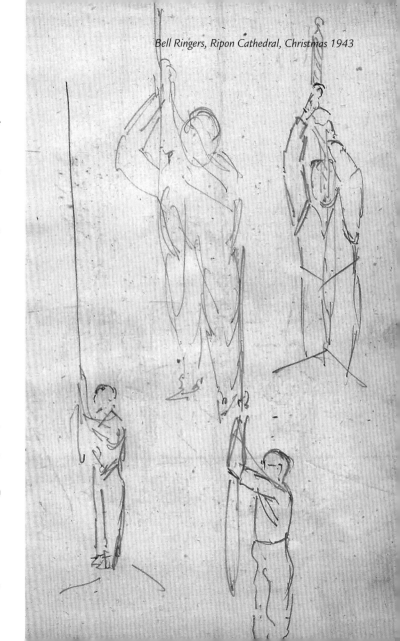

Bell Ringers, Ripon Cathedral, Christmas 1943

training period. Life was busy and long days were spent in training. One of the main courses was vehicle maintenance where a lot could be learnt about engines and detection of faults. Then there was the water proofing – essential because there were a number of landings from ships and also crossings of wide rivers in training for the invasion of Normandy. Very important was getting a vehicle on to firm ground from muddy fields or shell-pocked roads. Vehicles were deliberately bogged down for training, and all the larger trucks carried winching gear. Eventually, after plenty of practice, a vehicle could be moved within 15 minutes or so.

Artillery Troop Captains such as Julian went on observation courses, covering all types of targets, layout of gun positions and liaison with infantry and tanks. There were signalling and intelligence courses because officers were expected to operate the wireless sets and have the ability to notice any particular badges on prisoners, and recognise captured enemy maps and documents.

A typical weekly training schedule would include: gun drill for some, wireless set operating, driving instruction, map reading, gas mask drill, digging (plenty of this), Bren gun and rifle instruction, also use of the Sten gun, aircraft recognition, etc. "Stables" (maintaining the vehicles) every evening; then, after evening meal, about twice weekly, there was practice giving orders for the guns. Gunnery is a very mathematical science, and it was Julian's skill with numbers that served him well as a gunnery officer.

The orders for firing had to be given in a certain sequence; and, for barrages, all the details of ranges, times for shooting and rates of fire and the lifts, or alteration in range to cover more ground as the infantry moved forward, had to be calculated in advance – sometimes two days or so before zero hour. For greater accuracy, the effect of wind and humidity just before zero hour was sent to all gun positions and applied to the ranges already calculated. Knowing the exact position of the guns on the map, and the map reference of the target, the distance in yards or metres was worked out.

The target might be a small village or port or a town, a wood or farmhouse and buildings, or a railway junction and likely parking places for tanks and other vehicles. With wireless sets, all the guns (with those from other divisions, medium artillery and heavy artillery) received the order to fire at the same time. The orders would follow a pattern – the

barrage starting at a line for six minutes' firing, then lifting 100 yards for three minutes' firing so that the infantry could advance at a steady rate of 100 yards every three minutes. Obviously, if they went forward too quickly their own shells would hit them, so it was absolutely vital that the Infantry Officers and NCOs knew the details of the fire plan. The Artillery Forward Observation Officer would be close to the leading Infantry Officer and watch out for any shells dropping short, and he would then ask (via his wireless set or field telephone) for the Gun Position Officers to check the ranges on the guns.

During training there developed an intense feeling of mutual trust, affection and esteem between the infantry regiments and the batteries of the artillery regiments. The 181st always worked with the 44th Brigade, supporting the Infantry Regiments of 8th Royal Scots, 6th King's Own Scottish Borderers and 6th Royal Scots Fusiliers. They spent plenty of time together and knew each other well.

In March 1944, Julian was turning his thoughts to how his career would map out after the war was over. He drafted a letter to Sir Alan Rae Smith, the senior partner to whom he was articled at Deloitte's until 1939. He thought it wise to write then, as later may have been too late. Julian also wondered if he and his father ought to be doing something for Michael about his career – Michael being quite unable to communicate with the outside world from his Japanese POW camp in Thailand. "Another year, so Monty seems to think, may possibly see this European theatre of war over – then for the Japs," Julian added.

"Dear Sir Alan, I am writing to you now to enquire into my position as a one-time articled clerk. As you know, I should have taken my finals in October 1940, but I was called up on 1st September 1939 with the rest of the Territorials and I was unable to complete my time with Deloitte's. As so many people seem to be thinking ahead, perhaps some decision has now been reached by the Institute about finishing articles after the war and the question of qualifying as a Chartered Accountant. Everything depends on the next year's warfare; all being well I hope to be demobilised in my turn and I would like to know in that case how I stand.

"As this year is to be the final test of all that we have been working up to for the last four years, I feel it is perhaps presuming too much to look beyond instead of

concentrating on the things of the moment. But if I get through unscathed I shall count myself unprepared if I have not considered the period of the winding up of the War that will follow. It is probably going to be the hardest and the most important part of it.

"I have not been near London for over a year now, nor do I look like getting the opportunity for some time, otherwise I should have paid Deloitte's a visit. I expect most of my own contemporaries have been called up by now."

There is no record of Sir Alan's reply, but accountancy was to play no further role in Julian's life. However, his name is on the DPG War Memorial (now housed in the headquarters of PriceWaterhouseCoopers at London's Embankment Place); and also on the Roll of Honour at the Institute of Chartered Accountants at Chartered Accountants' Hall. Clearly, the Institute recognised Julian as a Member, even though he was unable to sit his final exams.

During this period of working in London and commuting from Hertfordshire Julian had few opportunities to get home to Brancaster. On his rare visits there was little time

'Here is a sketch of the Savoy… It has come out fairly well' (May 1944)

for sailing, although his subscription to Brancaster Staithe Sailing Club was kept up – the wartime rate being five shillings a year for members of the Club on active service. Once home, he still found time to paint. After one occasion in February 1944, he wrote to his father from North Yorkshire:

"I meant to write to you while I was at home to send you a small painting that I did of the Island [Scolt Head]. I went one fair afternoon to the Island with shoes and flannel trousers, no gum-boots. I waded through the trickle of water by the Nod and found the watcher's hut and Coast Guard's place deserted. So I sat down to paint just a watercolour.

"The way back was right in the direction of the hole where we fish, skating across the thin mud to those sandy marshes. But when I got to the shortest way across on to the Stone Banks Buoy I found the tide had not gone down far enough, so I had to wade up to the top of my legs and got drenched, so I slop-hopped across the flats straight home.

"The oil painting I did when I got back [see page 1]. What do you think of it? It is a bit small, but it was more or less an experiment. I happened to have the paints out for a small toy I made for Virginia. I don't suppose that will last long, as it was rather fragile!"

Julian's many interests covered the construction of model railways and wooden toy-making. He was a member of the Society of Model and Experimental Engineers, and attended meetings in London. A copy of the 1942 Evans Brothers book How to Make Strong Wooden Toys formed part of his collection.

In April 1944, Penguin Classics launched a series of slim paperback books – in landscape format with plain beige and white covers – called

'Penguin Modern Painters'. Edited by Sir Kenneth Clark, Director of the National Gallery, the first four were on Henry Moore, Graham Sutherland, Duncan Grant and Paul Nash. Susan sent a gift of some of the books to Julian after a rare visit to see him at his unit in May 1944.

During that trip, they danced together at The Savoy in The Strand (see page 37), a scene Julian recalled in a letter to his wife:

"Here is a sketch of the Savoy one I did. It has come out fairly well, but might be any of thousands of gleaming golden galleries for gallivanting and gangling goblets and guzzling goose and garlic!

"Thank you for the modern artist books that came today. Here is Duncan Grant for you. I think he is the best of the bunch. The one I want to get is Victor Pasmore, as he is mentioned in the Wilson Steer book as a similar painter. I read the Wilson Steer in the train until I dropped off to sleep.

"I got back to the Battery in time to change into a pair of shorts and to dash off on a four-mile trot round the countryside. Yesterday was the most vigorous day I have ever spent. We had a ten-mile march on hard roads and a little soft turf, but mostly hard roads. It is not the effort of doing it oneself that is so bad, but keeping everyone else up to the mark and making them go as fast as you can when you feel like falling out by the wayside. Really I am the laziest of them all, and would far sooner have been resting on green turf, painting the view, but one cannot say so.

"We set off in the evening to dig holes in the ground at three o'clock in the morning; after unearthing no end of flints, we filled them all in again. The best part of that evening's entertainment was doughnuts and tea at midnight. Extremely good also the nightingales who sang fervently although picks and shovels were making clanging noises against the flinty earth all around the wood where they sang. I have heard the nightingale at Knebworth but I have never heard several all singing together. I knelt on the wet grass hill above the wood and listened. He is a remarkable bird, but not as good as the blackbird in April, though. The stillness of the night air makes the nightingale famous, whereas the blackbird has to cope with all the day noises and stirrings that go on around him.

"We got in about four o'clock; I could scarcely swing a pick above my head when we were finally allowed to pack up.

"I suddenly thought yesterday that there might be something of financial value in some of my sketches and I wonder if it is worth doing something about it. Pictures are selling very easily now, and it might be a good thing to pour a little more into the coffers. What do you think? Do ask the sweet costume creature [he was referring to Sophie Fedorovitch, a Russian émigré who designed costumes for the London Theatre and later for Sir Frederick Ashton's Ballets, and who was a neighbour at Marsh Farm, Brancaster] what it is like now. I am completely out of touch and have never done anything in that way of trying to sell, except when I sent two pictures up to the London Group Exhibition that were not accepted. It was Fred Mayor in Cork Street who advised me to try, but he is away doing camouflage work somewhere.

"I'll look for a postcard album for you. I have seen a shop that has a lot more Penguin books of Modern Artists, but they were shut the last time I was there. I must try again. I still have done no local paintings here – and there are lots of lovely trees to do, and some good churches. Just how much one can get away with, though, I am not quite sure."

In March 1944, the Division was visited first by the King, then by Prime Minister Winston Churchill. Rumours abounded of a posting to India, with one gunner even shaving his head in preparation for the heat. Such speculation proved wide of the mark as the Division's first taste of action was to be much closer to home. By April 1944, the Regiment had moved to Worthing in Sussex, the Concentration Area for the allied invasion force. The artillery regiments were located between Ashington, Worthing and Lancing. On 14 May, Julian wrote to his father to thank him for a hand-made leather wallet of a montage of small family photographs:

"That is the most superb present I have ever had from you to take with me wherever I go. Thank you very much. All the photographs are so good. I was wondering how I was going to take the family portraits into battle. I feel that was the original idea of miniature portrait paintings that first flourished in Elizabethan days. I recognise the snippet of the terns photograph, one of the best. Did you sew up the seams yourself I rather wondered?

"Censoring letters is a new occupation for me, and takes up a good time every evening. They write reams sometimes, all about nothing, full of padding. It is a good line on their thoughts, though they seldom say anything against the army; I often wonder if they feel it. I don't think they do, because we have an Aunt Sally period occasionally at which I hear anything that they have to say.

Convoy, Normandy-bound, 14 June 1944

"They are a mixed bunch geographically, Inverness to Plymouth, Cardiff to Walthamstow. The best one is a sergeant from Welwyn, a most cheery man. We have long talks about Hertfordshire together. He is the only local I have – no one from Norfolk or East Anglia."

A few days later he wrote to Nanny Rees:

"I have had two lovely drawings of Juliet done by Joan Cochme, the newcomer to Cobblestones. They are so good, I am going to keep one with me. Where I shall carry it, I do not know. It is not quite so easy as that lovely set of photographs that Daddy did for me. I had a sweet letter from Clara at 'The Ship' thanking me for sending her and Maud a small book on horse brasses [see page 46]."

Around 8 June, the Regiment moved closer to Tilbury Docks. On 10 June, the officers and men were on their way to the docks with their French Francs and 'bags vomit' (sick bags). The Regiment was due to have started loading on the Sunday, but the dockers refused to work on their day off.

Julian's 177 Battery was due to join the US liberty ship Fort Biloxi. With guns, vehicles and men aboard, she sailed on the evening of 12 June. The next day she had joined the rest of the Regiment off Southend-on-Sea to await convoy. On 14 June, the convoy sailed for France. It was a smooth crossing, unopposed, and by 22.00 hours on the 15th they had anchored off Arromanches, with unloading getting under way almost immediately.

Julian wrote on sailing day in a letter home, the envelope marked 'Maritime Mail':

"Postcards will be the form I expect for a bit as we are pretty busy but just now I have some spare time. We got up at two o'clock yesterday morning and I felt very sleepy when we finished about 10 o'clock last night. I fear I shall be able to tell you little of what goes on but later I can enlarge considerably, so I shall have to remember it and in some weeks write and tell you all about it.

"Everything so far is alright. We have had a lot of hanging around and I have done no end of painting, chiefly of my favourite subjects [boats]. Then have had to fly around to get things done in time. Yes, I sometimes feel like a Crusader, and then again it is all like a big exercise, with everything perfectly normal, falling men in, and counting them

over to see if they are all there. Everybody is in extremely good form, and they have been all along. I had trouble with one Cockney who tried to go absent, not deserting, but just going home for the afternoon when we were really confined to camp."

"Everything is so ponderous so far, so gigantic, and on such a huge scale that one feels like a very small ant among it all. With everything done for one, and no orders to give or to receive, it seems a bit strange. Shortly after this intermediate step I think things will go with a swing again. Then I can get on with it. With the knowledge of the sights I have seen just within the last few hours, I cannot fail to see how 'This Business', as Monty himself calls it, can fail to be over by about Christmas – and then who knows what after that.

"Not an incident to report or relate even if I could tell you. I saw the most fascinating store cupboard yesterday: every conceivable type of food and utensil for living purposes – food from everywhere, every sort of tinned fruit and fish, meat and sauce. Things I have not seen in years. I lit and drank my first tin of self-heating soup the other day – the best idea in years. You merely pierce the holes in the top and light the fuse, which burns for about three minutes and the soup is piping hot. There is cocoa too, very rich and creamy. It cannot be put out no matter how bad the weather or wind – the soup is so good too.

"A word about money: I have settled with Barclays and sent them £100 from the National Provincial Bank. There is about £90 there in an emergency, on current account, and a further £30 on deposit. Neither is meant to be touched except for a real emergency."

On 15 June, Julian wrote to his mother:

"I can now say that we have been on board ship. Once the loading started [into a merchantman] it went very quickly. The Navy and Air Force must have been doing their jobs very well because we had no interference at all at any time, though the ship had been shelled on its previous voyage. I saw a little of the loading which was done very well but got the first glimpse of the boat itself when we took all the men down with their kits to embark. We were very encumbered and one wretched man slipped going up the gangway and could not rise to his feet [illustrated on page 48]. The whole convoy when finally arranged in their proper order was a terrific sight. I painted and sketched all day long in an effort to catch some of the sights, sights which I shall never be able to describe with the pen.

"So much journalese has been pouring out on the Second Front that a little correction to detail may be necessary, but I shall have to do that later as I can give no details now. I will say though how well treated we have been by the Merchant Navy. We have our own tinned rations and sleep where we can, but have been royally entertained by them at other times – Barclays Lager, canned, is the most popular entertainer (tell Daddy). There is nothing to tell about enemy action because there simply has not been any. I rather hoped to get some to see how people would behave. But no, the Navy and Air Force have silenced all that so it seems. That is why it is still difficult to come to earth and realise what one is about.

"Do please tell Daddy that the only sort of thing I require is an occasional sketch book or pencil and a spare No. 7 sable watercolour brush and a No. 4. These things are so hard to find, that they represent a very difficult problem. For pencils 'B' is best. We are so well equipped otherwise and I never smoke – that I cannot think of any other wants. But I will let you know at once if I do.

"This is all so vast that one cannot see the true magnitude of it – though if I look out through the porthole I can see a very good sight."

Things may have started well for 177 Battery, but they soon deteriorated. A huge storm hit the Normandy coast, described by many as the worst in living memory. Unloading of 178 and 179 Batteries proceeded with little trouble, but it was to be a different story for 177.

As unloading commenced, the wind was getting up and the sea had become rather choppy. However, they were able to quickly off-load 'Able' Troop's four guns, limbers and towing quads, together with Bren carrier, 14-hundredweight truck and Jeep, and then the landing craft ploughed safely to the beach. Also on board was the reconnaissance party of the commanding officer, second-in-command, signallers and other officers, including Julian, being 'Baker' Troop commander. They all had an easy landing and missed the coming storm and the problems it caused.

On 20 June, Julian wrote (with a Field Post Office postmark):

"We arrived in France safe and sound. The voyage itself was peaceful and calm and no sign of the enemy. I might have been sailing in 'Sanderling', straight into the beach, at low tide, off the Golf Course, it was so simple. It was a lovely sunny day with hot white dusty roads. A few Frenchmen still at their jobs – farming. Also the rest of the population were

Captain Jack Cunis, 'Echo' Troop Commander

riding about on bicycles in holiday mood — looking very flashy, in the case of the men, and rather attractive in the case of the girls who all wore dark sun-glasses."

Back at sea, a large Landing Craft, Tank (LCT) had to be lashed to the side of Fort Biloxi because of the storm. It broke free and the Battery lost two guns, various lorries and equipment for the Regimental HQ. The LCT was smashed on rocks. There are reports that a huge barge, a 'Rhino', came alongside Fort Biloxi and much more equipment was unloaded on to it, but the wind and sea were so rough that the Rhino – with vehicles and guns on it, including a dumper truck and concrete mixer – was swept away. The Rhino was a long, wide floating platform, built of steel pontoons joined together by steel angle irons. The larger barges had up to 500-ton capacity.

It was 21 June, when the storm eased, before the rest of the Regiment landed, farther down the coast at St-Côme-de-Fresné. The Regiment got back together at Brécy by 23 June, eight miles inland. There was considerable ribbing of, and embarrassment for, 177 Battery because it arrived without its guns. Certain planned actions were delayed while the unit was resupplied.

Parties searching the landing beaches for recoverable equipment were to find a collar marked 'Cunis'. Captain Jack Cunis was 'Echo' Troop Commander. He had landed earlier, before the problems, and only found out about the 'collar' story 50 years later!

The reconnaissance parties from the 181st that had landed at Arromanches before the storm looked around the area just north of Le Mesnil-Patry and Norrey-en-Bessin and had joint meetings with the infantry, tank and anti-tank units. Julian helped to decide the positions of the guns of 177 Battery at Brouay (misspelled in the Regimental War Diary as Bronay) and had the more dangerous task of finding suitable observation posts from which to watch for enemy movements.

On the edge of Norrey-en-Bessin, looking south across the fields, stood a row of burnt-out Canadian tanks, a raw reminder of the First Front that had reached that point after D-Day. There was some controversy regarding the siting of the artillery unit where German gunfire had already done so much damage, as they clearly had the range for the target and would

again bombard the position once the British guns had been established.

It was from a two-storey house adjacent to the church at Norrey-en-Bessin, standing well back from an upper window, that Julian and Major Archie Browne of 177 Battery could see towards their objective – St Manvieu. It would have been after just such a recce that Julian was able to write home for the last time:

"Today I went into a garden of a huge empty house lately occupied by some German troops and found a wilderness. But one half of the wilderness was a mass of lovely globe artichokes. I am going to have some for tea. I cut the six best I could find."

Had the unloading gone to plan, the Regiment would have moved into action on 18 June at Brouay as part of a divisional artillery assault. 'Operation Epsom' became known to the 15th Division as 'The Battle of the Scottish Corridor'. It was later renamed 'The Battle of the Odon' after the French river of the same name.

Julian continued in his last letter:

"After a heavy day's rain things look rather wet and drippy. We made a very poor effort at a tent with a sheet over some poles, so I changed everything round in the middle of a series of heavy showers, got some straw from a local farm and ate a huge meal, so that last night when we finally went off to sleep we were all warm and comfortable. But my clothes, which I hung up to dry, were dripping – so I got Barwick to get me a clean lot out. I still cannot realise that it is not an exercise. Everybody is in excellent form."

On 25 June, the 181st was shelled by German guns while located at the former Canadian position and three gun crew were killed, with three others seriously wounded.

With its replacement 25-pounders, 26 June saw 181 Field Regiment join more than 300 other field guns in action (plus hundreds of naval warship guns offshore), delivering a barrage of one shell every 10 seconds or so, which lasted for hours.

Robert Woollcombe, a platoon commander with the King's Own Scottish Borderers, had an "indelible memory" of the day which he recalls in some detail in his memoir: "The minute hand touched 7.30. ... On the second, nine hundred guns of all calibres, topped by the 15-inch broadsides from the distant battleships lying off the beaches, vomited their inferno. Concealed guns opened from fields, hedges and farms in every direction around us, almost as if arranged in tiers. During short pauses between salvoes more guns could be heard, and right away, further guns, filling and reverberating the very atmosphere with a sustained, muffled hammering.

"It was like rolls of thunder, only it never slackened. Then the guns near by battered out again with loud, vicious, strangely mournful repercussions. The thunder angry, violent and death-dealing. Hurling itself over strong-points, enemy gun areas, forming-up places, tank laagers, and above all concentrated into the creeping mass of shells that raked ahead of our own infantrymen, as thousands of gunners bent to their task. Little rashes of goose-flesh ran over the skin. One was hot and cold, and very moved. All this 'stuff' in support of us! Every single gun at maximum effort to kill; to help us."

B Troop 177 Battery, 2 June 1944 (Julian is in the centre of the second row, circled)

As a Forward Observation Officer, Julian would normally have been in a Bren carrier with his observation post assistant, the Bren gunner and a wireless operator (signaller), advancing with a company of the 6th Battalion Royal Scots Fusiliers. However, Major Maurice Cooke of the 8th Royal Scots recalls the evening of 25 June in his diary: "I went down to Battalion HQ for a final conference and as we came away I met Cory-Wright, the gunner. I asked him jokingly whether he was going to paint next day as he had spent many a dull hour on exercise with his watercolours. He smiled his cheerful, friendly smile and said 'it depended'. I also asked him how he was going to travel, in his Bren-carrier? He replied, 'no, he would walk, two men could carry the wireless set while a third worked it – it would make less of a target'."

On the morning of 26 June, Julian and his party began to move on foot (to avoid creating dust and making them an easier target) towards St. Manvieu in order to recce the Observation Post position. Captain Cunis was at the Command Post and he called Julian on the field telephone and asked how it was going at the front. "Pretty brisk," Julian replied – then the line went dead. A shell or mortar bomb had landed near Julian's party.

Sergeant Signaller John Bramald, accompanying him on the mission, recalled that the Captain's only concern was for his men: "Are you all right?" Julian asked, to which Bramald was able to reply, "Yes, sir", before his troop commander lost consciousness and died.

Julian, the first and only artillery officer lost in the action, was buried initially beside the shell hole where he was killed and later moved to the British Military Cemetery at Tilly-sur-Seulles. His passing is commemorated in Norfolk on the Brancaster Village War Memorial, on a brass plaque in the church of St Mary the Virgin and on the gates of the Royal West Norfolk Golf Club, where he spent so many happy days. He is also listed on the Knebworth War Memorial, on the Bronze War Memorial in the Colonnades at Eton College, and on the stone plinth and bronze plaque at Sandroyd school.

The Regiment was deeply saddened by his loss, and two weeks later

18th Green from the 19th, Royal West Norfolk Golf Club, Brancaster. Inset: Captain Julian Cory-Wright. Facing page: Memorial Gates to the Royal West Norfolk Golf Club, on which Julian is commemorated

the ripples spread among family and friends in Norfolk and beyond. At that time there were no personal visits to widows or mothers, and the official War Office telegram arrived at Congham Post Office while Susan was on a three-mile walk with the children. The local Postmistress was distraught at having to bear the sad tidings. On receiving the news, Susan left to visit Julian's parents. At this point, Geoffrey was working in Nottingham with the Ministry of Fuel and Power. A short note in Geoffrey's diary for 13 July 1944 reads: "Arrived in Nottingham and found Susan's telegram". A few days later, back in Brancaster, Felicity wrote to Geoffrey:

"Here memories crowd out grief sometimes and sometimes overwhelm me, but I am glad I came as I feel a little nearer to our darling though he still seems very far away cloaked in gold and light. I stare at his photograph and wonder almost if he was ever there and my heart aches for just one more sight of him coming through the green gate, bursting through the door or even striding far away over the marshes. I must learn not to yearn for the past and to be less selfish in my grief. I feel lost and dazed and only want to lie in the sand dunes and call his name to the silent marshes. I wish you were here with me but please don't think I am lonely. I can never be lonely if I let memories have their full fling and I don't want to crush them now in case they fade forever."

When summer was over, Susan decided to return to Northumberland and made the journey by train with three children, putting baby Richard, just six months old, in the luggage rack above the seats to sleep – the rope netting of the luggage rack made a comfortable cradle. They stayed with the Pumphrey family at Belsay where Susan and Julian had spent many happy hours together during his training. Iris Pumphrey, known affectionately to Susan and her family as "Mrs Mum", wrote in October 1944 to Felicity:

Photograph: Libby McCullough

"My dear Felicity, I have waited a long time to answer your darling letter of October 11th but not because I didn't love it, and haven't re-read it often. More because we are very busy and it is so difficult to 'toss off' a real letter – and now Susan and the babies have been here four weeks, I feel I know better the things you want to hear.

"First, they have been four weeks without one sign of anything but loveliness of character on Susan's side. My heart aches for her – she stares, tall and pale and still and the tears pour down her cheeks and she holds out a hand and twists her fingers round mine in a sort of agony of silence. At those moments when she says nothing I feel she is going really through Hell, poor darling. But when she is ordinary and happy, she speaks much of Julian, easily, adoringly and perfectly naturally.

"She is heavenly with the children, grave rather, quiet, patient and clever. Up in the nursery you see a delicious sight of the two little girls riding side by side on two rocking horses, gently talking while jogging along side by side just as tho' they were riding along a lane quietly discussing affairs. As for Richard, I never saw a more darling, amiable little boy – he is so merry, loving and sweet. It is heaven to have the nursery open again, twinkling fire, toys everywhere, garments airing on towel horses, and constant applications for new mugs, jam and biscuits.

"Mrs Hall, who idolised Julian, declines to take time off at all while they are here, and feeds them excellently, and there simply can't be any argument about that. She is a complete, devoted autocrat and we should all go short before the children. However, so far there has been no question of that as milk abounds and the rest is easy. So all seems to be going as well as it can.

"The loss is profound and never ever does one forget it. The whole sad world is so hard to face with courage. Oh how utterly natural and understandable that you should feel your gallant spirit flagging, your cup of courage empty. Julian is safe. How you must ache for Michael, far, far more remote he must seem than Julian is. I hope David and Jon won't go too soon. It is too much to bear. Do come and see us, Love Iris."

When Susan returned to Norfolk, with no home and very little money, her author aunt Honor Elwes provided Wensum House, East Rudham, for the little family to live in. "The perfect place in Norfolk," Susan wrote, "halfway between Congham and Brancaster." Indeed, it meant the children were only eight miles from both sets of grandparents.

Tributes poured in from Julian's lifelong friends who described him as the kindest and most understanding person. The sort of friendship he inspired was one that lasted long after they were all separated. Among Brancaster friends who had written was Evie Martelli, who said: "That beauty, innocence and gentleness that Julian's youth personified made me think always of Rupert Brooke and the 1914 poems. I shall never look across to the Island [Scolt Head] again without thinking of Julian, and particularly of that day when he faced danger with me as gallantly as he must have now."

Joan Evershed wrote: "It just doesn't seem possible that the notice in *The Times* is true. It's probably difficult for anyone who hasn't got sons to quite appreciate all they mean to parents, but having seen you and Geoff with the boys so much one got a good idea. And Julian being born in the last war while you were anxious about Geoffrey must have always made a difference to you. Why can't old devils like Raymond and I go and get killed instead of these young men who have had no time to live and could do so much in the world. He always seemed so untouched by all the dreariness that goes into many people's lives. One always pictured him at home on the marshes or on a boat. In time you will feel proud that he died fighting for England and his life was untarnished."

The Eversheds stayed at The Ship in Brancaster on their visits, which was run by Maud Wordingham and her sister Clara (pictured). On 14 July, Maud wrote to Felicity and Geoffrey: "May we all say how grieved and sorry we are about Master Julian. It is a great price you have paid for this awful

Clara Wordingham at The Ship, Brancaster

time we are living in. It's only such a short time since he was in and looking at Clara's brasses [which decorated the doorway at the back of the bar] and even remembering to send her a book about them. With all our sympathy to a very kindly and great family."

Late in 1944, Julian's tin trunk with his personal possessions was returned from France. It contained, among other things, his precious family photographs, the sketch of Juliet by Joan Cochme, his paint box and brushes, and the books of sketches he made at the start of that fateful voyage to Normandy. The dumper truck he drew being loaded on board the Fort Biloxi at Tilbury may never have made it on to the beaches of Normandy, but his sketch books got there and back.

The war hadn't quite finished for the Cory-Wright family. Even though Michael returned from imprisonment by the Japanese in late 1945, one of the twins, Jonathan, was killed while serving in Germany as a Lieutenant in the Scots Guards during the last months of the war. He died on Monday April 9 1945 and is buried in Rheinberg War Cemetery. (News of the deaths of his two brothers had reached Michael on the 'bush telegraph' during his imprisonment by the Japanese.) Jonathan's twin, David, a Captain in the Scots Guards, survived.

As with so many thousands of bright young men deprived of their futures in the greatest war against tyranny, we will never know what more Julian would have achieved. Loved as a son, husband, brother and father, he made a lasting impression during his 27 years, exemplifying the family motto *Dum Vivimus Vivamus*: "While we live – let's live!".

Thanks to his remarkable portfolio of paintings, drawings and prints, and to the determination of his family, Julian's journey from Norfolk to Normandy can be commemorated with much more than just words engraved on brass, bronze and stone. ∎

PORTFOLIO 1 Setting sail for Normandy

On board the US liberty ship Fort Boloxi, 14 June 1944: 'We have had a lot of hanging around and I have done no end of painting, chiefly of my favourite subjects'

'The whole convoy when finally arranged in their proper order was a terrific sight. I painted and sketched all day long in an effort to catch some of the sights, sights which I shall never be able to describe with the pen'

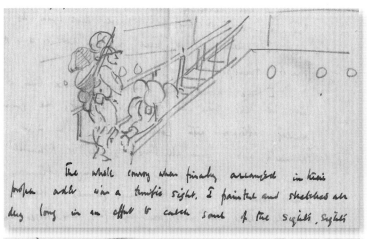

The whole convoy when finally arranged in their proper order was a terrific sight. I painted and sketched all day long in an effort to catch some of the sights. sights

Left: the embarkation incident referred to in Julian's letter home — 'We were very encumbered and one wretched man slipped going up the gangway and could not rise to his feet'. Below left: on board the Fort Biloxi. Below: sketch of laden ship ready to sail for Normandy. Opposite, clockwise from left: taking in the view; the convoy forms up; convoy in the Thames Estuary, D-Day + 8

Facing page: members of 177 Battery on board the Fort Biloxi. *Right: a dumper truck being loaded on board the Fort Biloxi at Tilbury Docks on 12 June 1944 – it was destined never to reach French soil, having been washed overboard during violent storms*

Above and facing page: sailing from the Thames Estuary for Normandy on 14 June 1944. 'Everything is so ponderous so far, so gigantic'

Top left: men of 177 Battery,181st Field Regiment leave Tilbury on the Fort Biloxi; Above: convoy in the Thames Estuary; Left and facing page: men of 177 Battery below deck

Landscape as seen from the deck of the Fort Biloxi

PORTFOLIO 2 **Training with the Royal Artillery**

60-pounder field gun, Ulgham Park, Northumberland, August 1940: 'We fired our guns today; very interesting. We were only firing into the sea.'

A typical weekly training schedule would include: gun drill for some, wireless set operating, driving instruction, map reading, gas mask drill, digging (plenty of this), Bren gun and rifle instruction, also use of the Sten gun, aircraft recognition, etc

ULGHAM PARK 1940.

Above: ambulance and other vehicles, field dressing station. Facing page: Royal Artillery, Ulgham Park, 1940

Above: Royal Artillery mess, Larkhill. Facing page, clockwise from top left: a convoy stops in Aynho, Northamptonshire, in February 1943; field gun on Ross Links near Bamburgh on the Northumberland coast, 8 July 1943; Newcastle Central station, midnight, April 1943; waiting for the train

Top left: playing
cards; Bottom left:
soldiers at rest:
Below: reading in
the mess

ARCHIE.

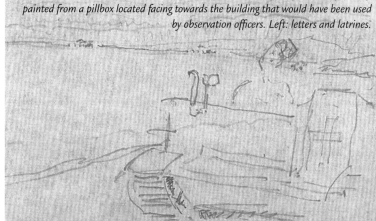

Bren carrier. Above: Major Archie Brown. Top left: Dunstanburgh Castle, probably painted from a pillbox located facing towards the building that would have been used by observation officers. Left: letters and latrines.

With 6RHA. 3/43

Top left: field gun emplacement.
Top right: soldiers resting under
a haystack. Above: Field Marshal
Montgomery during a visit to the
15th Scottish Division in Yorkshire,
February 1944. Far left: cap and
badge. Left: taking a break under the
trees. Facing page: signallers at their
sets at Divisional HQ, 1941

'Something's up ahead'. Facing page: 25-pounder field gun in a gun pit under camouflage — the gun pits were dug out by hand, taking four or five men about three hours to dig out a hole three to four feet deep

Top left: WVS Darlington canteen, February 1944. Above: Gunner Walker with his gas mask. Left: 'Stables' training every evening – maintaining vehicles. Facing page: Col. Rugge Price and RSM at a Regimental Command Post

From Norfolk to Normandy

Training with tanks

B.C. gives orders, 14 May 1942

Above: goodnight prayers by the camp bed. Top right: a camouflaged signals station.
Bottom right: map reading and motorbike. Facing page: soldiers repairing a vehicle

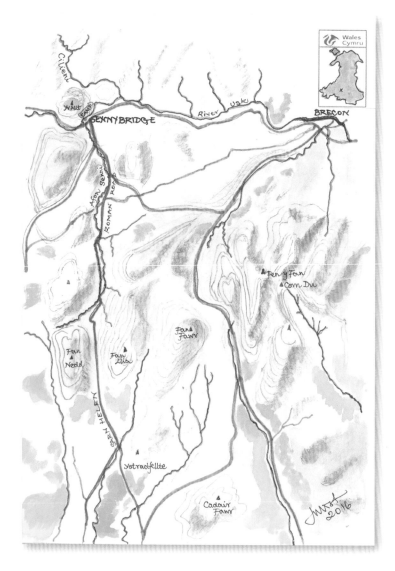

Between 8 and 22 June 1941, Julian's regiment was at RA Practice Camp, Sennybridge, near Brecon. It was from here that Julian painted a series of Cilieni Valley watercolours when he took off on a motorcycle with Emma to paint the scenery of that beautiful Welsh valley.

He wrote to his father:

"I spent most of yesterday on a motor bike painting and exploring. Yesterday evening, having decided to forgo dinner and stay out late still painting, I was asked in by a kind farmer and wife returning from the village to have supper with them. Tiny dark little farmhouse, but very good cider, boiled bacon, bread and butter. They all gabbled away in Welsh, and then apologised for doing so. The farmer I could never understand anyhow whether he spoke Welsh or English, but his wife was alright. An enormous cheese press occupied one side of the room and the fireplace the other. They were sweet people and very thrilled that they had an officer to supper."

Map: Juliet Webster
Facing page: Aber-llia near Ystradfellte – 'Over the top and down the other side'

Brecon Hills from a vantage point above the camp, June 1941

William Williams' farm at Gallt-y-bere in the Doethie Valley. Julian described the valley as 'where the kites nest'

'The one that got me my supper' — looking into Mr Tom Davies' farm

'Joins the one that got me my supper'

Nant Gwernol Valley, Llandovery, where the Hertfordshire Yeomanry participated in a night exercise around 10 o'clock on the evening of 20 June 1941

Cilieni stream flowing into the Usk, June 1941

Pentre-bach

Pentre'r Felin, evening, June 1941: 'Had to come down lower to get water for water pot'

Towards Fan Llia, a subsidiary summit of Fan Fawr in the Fforest Fawr section of the Brecon Beacons

From Norfolk to Normandy

'The Cilieni stream where Emma and I crossed'

'Little pink house', Llandovery, Towy Valley

PORTFOLIO 3 Brancaster and North-West Norfolk

Brancaster Staithe, August 1936

Julian's birthdays were celebrated in Brancaster during the summer holidays, where he could indulge his passions for walking (usually with his poodle Emma), sailing, playing golf at the Royal West Norfolk Golf Club and, of course, painting

Brancaster from Scolt Head Island – a watercolour produced in preparation for the oil painting featured on page 1

Brancaster Harbour and the marshes, as seen from The Hoe

'Spirit of Brancaster' pastiche showing 'The Amity', a famous local boat that took part in the evacuation of Dunkirk. The vessel was still afloat as recently as the mid-1990s. Facing page: Brancaster marshes

Whelk houses, Brancaster Staithe — painted across two pages of Julian's sketchbook

Brancaster Staithe (crayon), 1930s

Harry Loose of the well-known local fishing family, Brancaster Staithe, 1941. Harry is painted near his mussel wash pit

Burnham Overy Staithe

From Norfolk to Normandy

Brancaster Staithe towards Scolt Head Island

Brancaster marshes and the clubhouse of the Royal West Norfolk Golf Club. Below left: the Watchbox at Brancaster Staithe; Below right: Wreck of 'The Lion', with Marsh Farm Barn behind — 'The Lion' had been used for unloading colliers, and got stuck on the marsh; it was eventually towed away for scrap

Brancaster Dial House and Barn. In the foreground is the converted lifeboat that was the first HQ of Brancaster Staithe Sailing Club

Facing page: fishermen's sheds. Top left: Brancaster mussel pits.
Middle left: The Hoe from the marshes. Bottom left: a Norfolk
church. Above: Julian at Brancaster with Emma

Denver Sluice, September 1936. Facing page: Burnham Market playing field

Castle Acre. Facing page: Bill Adams' traction engine, August 1942

The Granaries, Thornham, May 1936

Facing page, from top left clockwise: interior, The Hoe, Brancaster Staithe; Valley Farm Lane, Burnham Deepdale, August 1943; view from The Hoe, August 1943; St Mary's, Brancaster. Above: buoy on the shore, Burnham Deepdale

PORTFOLIO 4 **Knebworth and the Manor House**

The Manor House, Knebworth

'This fine old house, a Dower House on the Estate, is to be let. It is surrounded by lovely old grounds including tennis and croquet lawns, rose gardens, etc, and comprises hall, dining and drawing rooms, ten bedrooms, two bathrooms, kitchen, servants' hall, butler's pantry and other conveniences. Stabling and double garage. Rent £220 a year.'

Knebworth Barns, 1930s

The barns in the autumn

Knebworth Church. Facing page: Knebworth Park, 1937

The Wilderness, Knebworth Park (pastel on black paper), 1936. Facing page: a different artistic treatment of the same location

Facing page, from left: the Lake, Knebworth; farm buildings, Knebworth, 1930s. Above: Knebworth House Garden, 1936

From Norfolk to Normandy

PORTFOLIO 5 London and Eton

Tug and London Bridge from the East, with cranes, ships and davits, Fishmongers' Hall, the dome of Canon Street Station and Southwark Bridge beyond

Life in London meant more paintings and drawings of the capital, with Julian applying for permission from the Port of London Authority to paint in the London docks. The condition attached was that he should show them his work before exhibiting or publishing it.

From Green Park, London (pencil sketch). Facing page: a watercolour of the same scene

Brixton Road 17-Feb 37

London by Night. Facing page: a pen and ink sketch of the Brixton Road from J. C. Gambles Wholesale Chemist, 17 February 1937

Eton College Chapel.
Facing page: School Field, Eton

Eton Officer Training Corp – toast for tea. Facing page, from left: The Jordan, Eton; theatre mementos from Julian's 1939 scrapbook; The London Apprentice public house on the Thames at Isleworth

From Norfolk to Normandy

THE DISTRICT MESSENGER & THEATRE TICKET CO. LTD.

THEATRE TICKETS

Get your Seats from us AND SEE

Please examine your tickets and verify date, name of Theatre, &c. and whether Matinee or Evening, as mistakes cannot afterwards be rectified

PHONE TEMPLE BAR 1023

Telephone:
ROTtingdean
9333

"BELLA VISTA"
LONGRIDGE AVENUE,
SALTDEAN, SUSSEX

1940.

Dr. to Mrs. J. ROSE

BOARD RESIDENCE   BED & BREAKFAST

D.P.G.
4. iii. 36.

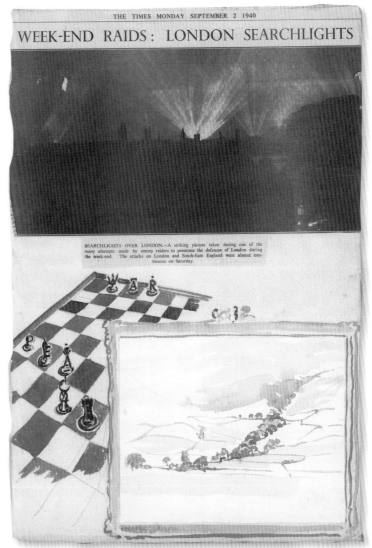

THE TIMES MONDAY SEPTEMBER 2 1940

WEEK-END RAIDS : LONDON SEARCHLIGHTS

SEARCHLIGHTS OVER LONDON.—A striking picture taken during one of the many attempts made by enemy raiders to penetrate the defences of London during the week-end. The attacks on London and South-East England were almost continuous on Saturday.

Facing page, from left: D.P.G 1936; chessboard and landscape from Julian's 1940 scrapbook. Above: the old London Bridge from the South Bank, looking towards the 1930s Shell Mex building. Right: Port of London permit. Far right: Julian produced this pencil sketch of the north-west steeple of St Paul's Cathedral from the second floor of a building in Paternoster Row while on an auditing job for Deloitte's c. 1937

PORT OF LONDON AUTHORITY

TO BE SURRENDERED

Issued

8th August, 19 38

Admit Mr. J. Cory-Wright

to the Authority's Docks and River Piers for the purpose of sketching general exterior scenes. Sites to be agreed with for the purpose of the Authority's officers.

available until 31st December, 1938.

To be presented to Police Officer at dock entrance or River Piermaster.

Public Relations Officer

Attention is called to the Conditions endorsed on the back hereof.

*A view from high up on Lower Thames Street looking across to the Tower of London,
the docks and the north span of Tower Bridge*

PORTFOLIO 6 Travels, trees and landscapes

Salisbury Cathedral

Julian was as bewitched by art as by sailing, and in July 1937 he and a friend Martin Russell travelled by train to Bavaria and Austria. Other painting excursions saw him visit Pembrokeshire in Wales, while even RA training provided landscape painting opportunities in the Lake District, Northumberland and Wiltshire

Walkern Mill, Hertfordshire, spring 1938. Facing page: trees by a river

Austrian landscape (watercolour and pencil). Facing page: unfinished watercolour of the Pilgrimage Church of St. Wolfgang, Wolfgangsee, Austria, July 1937

Watercolour mountain scene. Facing page, from left: Maria Gern Church; Pilgrimage Church of St. Wolfgang, Strobl

Bluebells on Skomer. Facing page: Julian's twin brothers, David and Jonathan, on Skomer with bluebells

Below and facing page: steep cliffs of Skomer Island, both watercolours (the first on grey sugar paper)

'The Fisherman's Hut'

Mill wheel and stream

The bridge at Lechlade

PORTFOLIO 7 Linocutting and linocuts

Wharf Scene, linocut

Julian's Eton years saw him develop an interest in linocutting. This method of relief printmaking allowed for inexpensive production of designs using the common household flooring material, some cutting tools and ink for creating a reverse impression of the image. Julian took the time in 1934 to produce his own hand-made guide to linocutting

Burnham Overy Boathouse (used as a Christmas card). Facing page: Scolt Head Island.
Overleaf, from left: Scallop Shell design; Shrimp in Net design; Curled Feather design

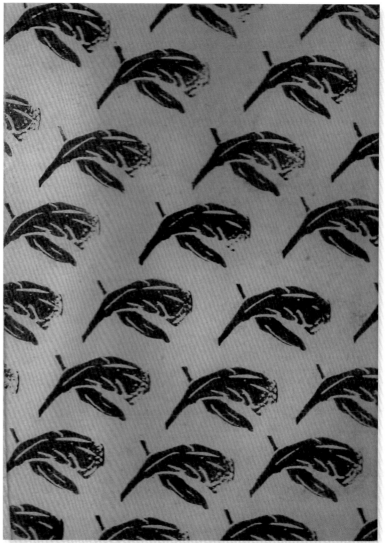

Left: The Churchyard Under Snow. Above: The Nile. Facing page, from left: an extract from Julian's linocutting instruction book; Blackfriars Bridge; The Poplars

A SHORT SURVEY OF PRACTICAL LINO-CUTTING.

LIST OF ILLUSTRATIONS. (WITH NOTES.)

Frontispeice.... "A Wharf Scene."

This ia a small section of a picture that
originally measured 12" by 8".Three seperate
blocks were used.The effect of the grey block
is good,and many different arrangments of sky
can be attempted with careful manipulation.

1.............. The Provost's garden from the Wall,Eton.

This particular proof shows to advantage
the way in which thin white lines can be used
to best effect.From the design point of view,
the background rather overshaddows the foreground.
nevertheless,a strong spenge of sunlight is
to be felt.

2............. "The Churchyard under snow."

This is a two block lino-cut,whose only
claim to mention,if the texture of the grey,
which has come out well.I doubt if the whole
effect would have been bettered,if the grey
had been a matt colour.

3........... "The Nile."

A good example of the way in which much
effect of light can be obtained with a clean
simply arranged design.This proof was obtained
by the professional method,a printing-press.

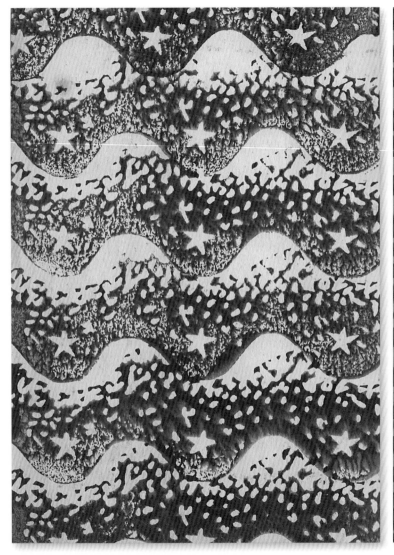

From Norfolk to Normandy

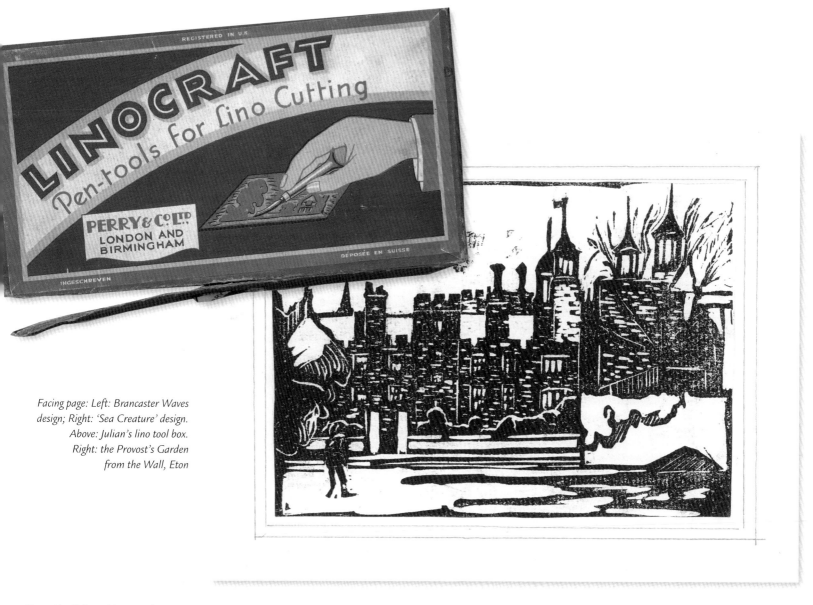

*Facing page: Left: Brancaster Waves
design; Right: 'Sea Creature' design.
Above: Julian's lino tool box.
Right: the Provost's Garden
from the Wall, Eton*

From Norfolk to Normandy

ACKNOWLEDGEMENTS

With thanks to Sir Hereward Wake, Bt., M.C., D.L., Major David Jamieson, V.C. and family, David Parsons and family, Hamilton-Baillie family, Major George Mann, John Butterwick, Lavinia, Marchioness of Cholmondley, Tom Stokes (177/181 Fd. Regt.) Major Dudley Shaw, D.S.O., Lord Campbell of Croy, Brigadier K.A. Timbers, Royal Artillery Historical Trust, Lt. Col. J. D. Sainsbury, T.D., F.S.A. of the Hertfordshire Yeomanry Historical Trust, John Hindle of 5th Division Workshop, Maurice Cooke (8th Btn. Royal Scots), Col. B. A. Fargus, O.B.E., (Adjutant of 8th Bn. The Royal Scots 1943/5), Major Jeremy York, Shropshire & Herefordshire Light Infantry, G. Archer Parfitt, KSLI Historical Trust, Reverend David Cairns (Padre, 131 Fd. Regt. R.A.), Major C. Brown, Records Officer, H.Q. Scots Guards, Sir Timothy Colman, Grace Attewell, the Briggs family, The Mayor Gallery, Phil Philo, David Napier, The National Trust, Audrey Earle, Bob Chestney, Peter Simkins, Imperial War Museum, Eton College, Coopers & Lybrand, PWC, The Library of the Institute of Chartered Accountants of England & Wales, Major Jack Cunis, Cyril Southerland, The Everitt family, Don Neal, Brigadier J L Pownall OBE, Knebworth PCC, Brancaster PCC, Brancaster Staithe Sailing Club, Madame Farquharson, Shirley Saunders, Royal West Norfolk Golf Club, David Brooksbank, The Ship Hotel Brancaster, Nick Smith of Picture This, Sandroyd School, Lt. Col. Tim Cole, Royal Artillery Association, Lt. Col. Robin Broke, General The Lord & Lady Dannatt, Alister and Verily Borthwick, Muckleburgh Collection, R G Carter Group, Royal British Legion, Veterans Norfolk, Jamie Athill, Deepdale Information and Visitors Centre, Stephen Crighton, Jane Macfarlane, Mel Clark, Lyn Weal, Vanessa Lubach, Herbie Slaughter, H. J. Jackson, The Dean and Chapter Norwich Cathedral, Chris Minchin, Paul Fenner, Shoemakers Arms Pentre-bach, Sara Fox & Jane Hand, Rhandir-mwyn & District Community Association, Ordnance Survey, The Clan Trust, Dickon Leigh-Wood, Antoine & Isabelle Riaux.

CORY-WRIGHT FAMILY TREE

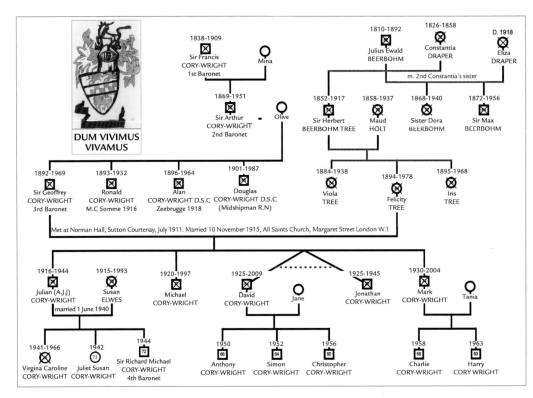

Further reading

Guns and Bugles: the Story of the 6th Bn K.S.L.I. – 181st Field Regiment RA 1940-1946. Don Neal, Brewin Books, 2001.

The History of the 15th (Scottish Division) 1939-1945. Lt. Gen. H. G. Martin, William Blackwood & Sons, 1948.